D0250664

Brilliance in 140 Characters or Less

Edited by Nick Douglas

With a Foreword by Biz Stone

The editor would like to thank the hundreds of Twitter users who contributed to this book; Biz Stone and his wonderful colleagues at Twitter; the fantastic agent Luke Janklow; and the talented people at It Books, including editor Kate Hamill, interior designer Ashley Halsey, cover designer Milan Bozic, and publicist Vanessa Schneider. Special thanks also to Rachel Fershleiser for her help and advice, and to Jay Hathaway and Cole Stryker for answering, over and over, the same question: "Is this funny?" Thanks to all of you, it finally is.

Have you written something witty on Twitter? Submit it to Twitter Wit at TwitterWit.net.

*it*books

FIRST EDITION

Designed by Ashley Halsey

Library of Congress Cataloging-in-Publication Data is available upon request.

ISBN 978-0-06-189727-6

09 10 11 12 13   OV/RRD   10 9 8 7 6 5 4 3 2 1

ABOUT THE AUTHOR

Technology writer and humorist NICK DOUGLAS was the founding editor of Valleywag.com, and has also written for *Wired*, Slate, and the Huffington Post. Douglas lives in New York City. Visit his website TooMuchNick.com.

itbooks

AN IMPRINT OF HARPERCOLLINSPUBLISHERS

FOREWORD

It's easy to assign less weight to a pun than a poem—after all, laughter lightens the load. However, the significance of humor as a delivery mechanism for important information should not be underestimated. Satirist Stephen Colbert called Twitter "the answer to the question you didn't know you had until you had the answer." In poking fun at this new form of communication, Mr. Colbert highlighted the very essence of innovation; breakthroughs like Twitter often occur by happy accident.

In the past decade, something interesting has been happening. People have been moving their electronic communication from closed systems like e-mail to open systems like social networks. There's more value in messages shared publicly because more opportunities arise. A kind of social alchemy takes place when a seemingly valueless message finds its way to someone for whom it strikes a chord. Lead can be turned into gold on an open communication network.

Simple, rudimentary exchanges of information between individuals in real time enables a flock of birds to move around an object in flight as if they were one organism. Speed and simplicity work together to create something of beauty. There are over a billion Internet users on this planet but there are four billion people with access to mobile texting. Twitter blends these networks with speed and simplicity and opens the combination to development. That means more opportunities for beauty—and well-timed zingers.

The first weekend we began experimenting with the concept of Twitter, I was tearing carpeting from the floor of my home in Berkeley, California. It was a hot day and my back was aching. My phone buzzed in my pocket. It was a tweet by my friend and long-time collaborator Evan Williams: "Sipping pinot noir in Sonoma after a massage." The striking difference between our two activities in that moment made me laugh out loud. When I realized our experiment was making me laugh, I knew it had potential.

We've seen people use Twitter to help each other during disasters, to break incredible news, to raise money for charities halfway around the world, to organize protests, to fight injustice, and simply to have fun. Through it all, there has been quickness, grace, simplicity, and humor—there has been wit. No matter how sophisticated the system becomes, it will never be about algorithms and machines. Wit is a powerful reminder that Twitter is not about the triumph of technology; it's about the triumph of humanity.

However, Oscar Wilde famously wrote, "It is a curious fact that people are never so trivial as when they take themselves seriously." As powerful as this system has the potential to be, we'd be nowhere without a good dose of funny. Humor makes life worth the effort. If everyone were serious all the time, I'm pretty sure we'd never get any work done. We're hiring pretty aggressively at our company these days, and key factors we look for are a good sense of humor and an active Twitter account.

Some of my favorite tweets are those that make me laugh all over again each time I revisit them. My friend Philip is an incredibly brilliant person. He's a musically and mathematically gifted serial entrepreneur with a goofy laugh and an impressive array of idiosyncrasies. He's also very tall and quintessentially geeky. In the middle of the night he Twittered, "Taking a bath. Come over if you want to learn about water displacement." It wouldn't surprise me to learn that he was prepared to discuss fluid mechanics with anyone who responded.

Wit is a wonderful word to associate with something that may turn out to be a favorable mutation in the evolution of human communication. Sharp, quick, inventive, and intelligent, with a natural aptitude for words, ideas, and humor: The very definition of wit brings to mind the people with whom I share my days. The heart of Twitter is the small team of folks working out of a loft in San Francisco, but our soul is made up of everyone around the world sharing, discovering, and building on this service.

A spark of genius from my friend and cofounder Jack Dorsey has transmuted from a simple idea to something mysteriously powerful. Given a limit of 140 characters, people consistently reaffirm that creativity is a renewable resource. It's easy to dismiss this simple new format upon first introduction, but tune in to the right frequency and you'll enter a world this book's curator wanders as a curious explorer. Keep your wits about you and enjoy this collection of Twitticisms. Nick worked hard to harvest the best.

Biz Stone (biz), Cofounder
Twitter, Inc.

INTRODUCTION

"Twitter," said user Henry Birdseye—or, on Twitter, tehawe-some—"is that friend you can turn to and say, 'This is bullshit,' when there's no one else around."

Of course, Twitter is plenty more. Technically, it's simply a social network where millions of users send text-message-length status updates to a list of "followers." As a simple platform for sharing messages of up to 140 characters, Twitter makes no demands of genre or intent. Since it began in 2006, the only guideline on the site is the prompt, "What are you doing?"

The most interesting users ignore that. The Twitter format serves a few forms of information particularly well: on-the-spot news updates, or questions like, "Anyone know a lawyer?" It's particularly great for whining or bragging. But the perfect use of Twitter, what the platform is practically destined for, is the witty one-liner.

Comedy *always* takes too long. The easiest way to improve any joke is to shorten it. And Twitter makes you do that. Even the British comedian Russell Brand (rustyrockets) has snipped out the spaces between words, struggling to fit a three-sentence joke into 140 characters. One of my favorite Twitter gags is just seven words long: "You know what this guitar needs? Lessons" (Tony_D). Twitter is the modern haiku, albeit with fewer cherry blossoms and more wisecracks. Brevity is, here, the soul of wit.

The tweets in this book came from hundreds of users. Anyone can write one particularly funny tweet. That's the democratic beauty of the one-liner. But some people turn Twitter wit into an obsession. They hit the star next to other people's funny tweets, so the tweets show up on third-party sites like Favrd and Favotter. Every day Favrd shows the most-starred tweets, drawn from a growing pool of hundreds of star-conscious Twitter users, not just as a popularity contest but as a way to find more wits to follow. The Twitter wits chasing these stars often meet in person. Avery Edison and Abby Finkelman (aedison and clapifyoulikeme) met on Twitter, then got engaged over it. Scott Simpson, Merlin Mann, and Adam Lisagor (scottsimpson, hotdogsladies, and lonelysandwich) started a comedy show online called "You Look Nice Today." And, of course, this book wouldn't be here without the contributions of hundreds of witty Twitterers.

The Twitter wits don't consider themselves an Algonquin Round Table, no matter how many times I try to label them as such. But Round Table member Dorothy Parker's assessment of New York's casual club of comedians applies to funny Twitter users as well: "Just a bunch of loudmouths showing off, saving their gags for days, waiting for a chance to spring them." Of course, then Ms. Parker says, "It was the terrible day of the wisecrack, so there didn't have to be any truth." That's not true of the Twitter wits. During the 2008 presidential election, they spread a populist kind of political commentary. When Sarah Palin announced her daughter's pregnancy, John Gruber (gruber) Twittered, "The press should only pay as much attention to this story as they would have if, say, Chelsea Clinton had gotten pregnant at 17." These back-row-of-the-country remarks, which feel like Jon Stewart's *Daily Show* commentary in real time, climaxed in Scott Simpson's verdict on the second presidential debate: "That won."

Of course, in daily life, the one-liners aren't anything more than a joke and a stress reliever. *The Office*'s Jim Halpert has a camera to grimace at. The rest of us have Twitter. We commiserate about our families, our jobs, our personal foibles. Even celebrities find a release. Comedian Stephen Fry (stephenfry) is a particularly masterful whiner. Plenty of British comedians found a new and loving audience on Twitter. But Mr. Fry is the only one so far to entertain tens of thousands with live updates about being stuck in an elevator, while his cross-dressing colleague Eddie Izzard (eddieizzard) has explained to his followers the balance between Girl Mode and Boy Mode.

Some users take on an alternate persona, like the whimsical TheLordYourGod, the sarcastic HotAmishChick, and the self-assured FakeSarahPalin. Some craft elaborate fictions, like Fireland's tweet (my personal favorite): "Why should I be the one to take the kids to see their psychologist? I don't even love them!" Most wits simply draw from daily life, using a hiccup or a bad fortune cookie as an excuse for a joke.

I now follow more than eight hundred people on Twitter. I don't recommend that—there's no way to keep up—but it's satisfying to bathe in the site's rich variety of comedy, and whom could I un-follow when everyone's so entertaining? I can't read everything that pours into my Twitter feed, so I'm dumping it on you. This book, three years in the making, covers the whole history of Twitter from its early days as a geek hangout to its current golden age as the world's hottest social network. It shows how clever a simple sentence can be, whether written by a renowned comedian, a college student, or a stay-at-home mom. And it's a chance to sit back from the torrent of tweets online and read a few that deserve some extra attention.

This is no exclusive club. Anyone can follow the hundreds of contributors in this book, read their tweets, and star them to show their appreciation. And anyone can use Twitter a little more sharply, turning a mundane status report into a witty aside. When you do, be sure to let me know.

Nick Douglas
(nick)

twitter wit

What's the deal with deaf people? Like, HELLO?

aedison

My half-brother has spent twenty-five years saying "Marijuana's not addictive!" Now he's shortened it to "Where's my phone?"

johnroderick

It's the postproduction phase of eating fast food that takes the experience all downhill.

feliciaday

I attribute most of my good days to a couple of people with voodoo dolls canceling each other out.

TBMimsTheThird

Bummer: Found out today the faithful dog I had as a boy was only CGI'ed in.

bonisteel

London city airport. Where form meets function. AND THEY HAVE A FIGHT.

stephenfry

I haven't had anything left for Lent since 1993 when, at Arsenio's urging, I gave it up for Marlon Wayans.

weselec

That's ok. I've been meaning to clean that table with a full glass of water for a while.

fedge

I wish LA was really as pretty as they made it look in "Blade Runner."

Tony_D

It's happened: I have developed real emotions for my iPhone. Actually, it's no surprise, because I was raised by a TV and a microwave.

stuartpaap

I get really uncomfortable when people ask embarrassing questions about sex. Like: "Is that it?"

nostrich

They should really start teaching young girls in school just how valuable their virginity is and the websites where you can legally sell it.

Yayaa

My 9yo hopes Santa brings a PS3. He'll be comforted to know the box of disappointment under the tree has another year of free rent inside.

joeschmidt

Haven't shaved in so long that I scratched my cheek and an ex-girlfriend tumbled out. No, that's a tapeworm.

pagecrusher

Whenever I see the word "Chicagoland" I envision a cold theme park where everyone is eating sausages and looks like Mike Ditka.

riebschlager

Doc says I'm as healthy as a horse. Well, a horse that smokes. But still.

sflovestory

I GET THE
IMPRESSION THAT
THE FAT ACCEPTANCE
MOVEMENT IS MORE
ABOUT ACCEPTANCE
THAN IT IS ABOUT
MOVEMENT.

strutting

Fauxboes: The annoying kids on Haight Street that endlessly harass you for money.

RSAndersen

I'm sure the gin we drank last night was off. Feeling a bit ill this morning. The tequila might have been off too. And the cocktails.

kerry_anne

I've got my health! Woo-hoo. (My grandmother was totally right.)

mulegirl

I am talking about music, which is a series of sounds they put behind television advertisements in your country.

warrenellis

I fell victim to a Fonzie scheme. My financial advisor kept flashing me the thumbs-up and saying "Aaaaay!" And calling me "Richie."

rsmallbone

Every morning I wake up and think, "Don't let it slip about Darth Vader being Luke's dad." It's hard having a 5 yr old who doesn't KNOW.

anitan

"Did you just fart?" "Well, I didn't *just* fart; there was pageantry and tradition."

Notactuallyme

So many input boxes. Ever go to search for a girl on Facebook and set her name as your status instead? Yeah, I just did that.

robinsloan

We are men of coffee, sleep does not become us.

aragszxki

Oh so we have to be all cryptic and call them "magic" brownies but we can come right out and say pot pie?

delfie

Dear McDonald's: I don't care *who* sings it, there is no such thing as "that McNuggets lovin'." Ew ew ew ew ew.

dbecher

This is embarrassing, but I didn't even know there was a country called Madagascar 2.

sloganeerist

The word "goodnight" makes my 1-yr-old cry, so I've had to rewrite some bedtime stories. "Howdy, Moon!"

irreverend

I always cheer myself up by crushing poor people's dreams at the last second on eBay. I can't think of a better reason to steal an identity.

DieLaughing

Doctor this afternoon: "Ever have thoughts of hurting yourself?" Me: "Nope." Doc: "Any idea why not?"

krabigail

The face-painting at the birthday party this morning was subpar. One girl asked for Tiger and got Surprised Basketball instead.

bcompton

Trust me. You do not want to see how a sausage fest is made.

biorhythmist

You can pretty much sell anything to me if your commercial uses the words "soothes" and "penetrates."

Jessabelle2o7

Congratulations. You fulfilled your biological imperative. Now make it stop touching me.

moonlet

Stop coming by unannounced. "Drop by anytime!" is just one of those things you say but don't mean, like, "You look great!" or "I love you."

shoesonwrong

OUR LAST WEEK OF SHOWS BEFORE A BREAK. DAVID BLAINE WILL BE IN THE AUDIENCE TONIGHT—I GUESS HE'LL BE BURIED UNDER THE HOUSE SEATS.

PENNJILLETTE

A modest proposal: Will you kind of marry me?

zdarsky

If you step in a pile of warm cat puke with bare feet, be prepared to clean up two piles of warm puke, only one of which is from a cat.

eclaggs

Until they produce a sweeping epic called "Canderel," "Sweet and Lowdown" has to be the film that sounds most like a sugar replacement.

biche

During sex ed in Catholic school, I was told an orgasm feels like how you feel just after a sneeze. This cold is great!

thepartycow

Uggs: the onomatopoeia of footwear.

poeks

I fought the bra and the bra won.

bliccy

The conference room I booked for a meeting just accepted. Is it wrong to reply, "I look forward to being inside you soon"?

idontlivehere

Today's efficiency level is stuck on "trying to scrub off a freckle."

eoporto

I have a theory. Close your eyes, walk into Whole Foods, and put random items into your cart. It always comes out to $45 a bag.

kevinrose

I prefer to be called a "person of thyroid."

urbanhipster

All 7-year-olds have good hustle.

apelad

Overheard walking out of a diner in Chelsea as snow started: "Ooooh! Fluffy white flakes!" Second guy to first: "Us? Or the snow?"

skydiver

He regrets teaching me how to cook, because now when he cooks, he does everything wrong.

CcSteff

Apparently "You don't have an interview somewhere else, do you?" is the new "You look nice today."

EntropyAS

At my funeral I want people to still be laughing at how it all happened.

SeoulBrother

Save your breath.
You're gonna
need it to
inflate your
girlfriend.

smartasshat

I put the PEN in "Penis." On a related note, it is amazing how well my underpants absorb blood.

bortflancrest

One night Kid Gleason says to me, "Merks, it's either the glove or the bottle." Course I picked the glove. Figured it held more whiskey.

loumerkin

Anyone who says "Frisco" gets their sourdough rations revoked and is forced to wear an Alcatraz Swim Team pullover all week.

rickabruzzo

The thing I don't like about masturbation is that you can't tell if you won.

scottsimpson

I told a lady once that she was prettier than the Venus de Milo. "How so?" she asked. "For one thing," I said, "you have arms."

thewesterly

I met a twelve-year-old Chinese sweatshop laborer and all I got was this lousy T-shirt.

cabel

Potty training is totally the Big Boss level at the end of age-two parenting.

mathowie

Gentlemen, I have some troubling news. Contrary to our longstanding assumption, it now appears that there is *nothing* beyond bed & bath.

nevenmrgan

The three worst mistakes you can make are overpromising and underdelivering.

dwineman

If he's a Smooth Operator, and I'm a Maneater, what hope is there for us?

pwilson720

The Election

While Twitter users can be found all along the political spectrum, the wittiest skewed toward Obama in 2008, registering their support in the form of one-liners. Word is, that worked out for them.

Obama's fighting dirty now. He'll use his "everybody who loves America, raise your hand high over your head!" tactic in the first debate.

FarkerPeaceboy

I was watching PBS, but turned to CNN, because they've got the "tardometer" that tracks the responses of uncommitted voters.

jason_pontin

I agree w/ John, it's time to fire the head of the SEC. COLLEGE FOOTBALL IS UNCOMPETITIVE & other regions deserve a chance!!

FakeSarahPalin

My brother: "I don't need an Obama bumper sticker. I drive a Prius."

joeschmitt

That won.

scottsimpson

Pro tip: Naming your auto repair establishment "Rim Job" isn't nearly as witty as you think and might end up, er, biting you in the ass.

wryredhead

Don't hurt him, Hammer. Just distract him. That's the plan.

bridgman

I'm off to LA to shoot a commercial and snort cocaine off the back of other, hotter commercials!

yuribaranovsky

The good thing about jury duty in DC? There's always a chance you'll be trying a member of the Bush administration.

anamariecox

Ragtime is the worst genre of music to get a hand job to.

ed_x

Productivity tip: Do everything faster.

carlmorris

I'm pretty sure every third bark translates to human as dumbass.

ChiNurse

I just passed a billboard in Wyoming that read "Earth's Final Days Are Happening!" As an early warning system that seems a bit ineffective.

elizabethlittle

My inner critic is voiced by Jon Lovitz. He's surprisingly affordable.

toldorknown

Circumstance dictates that I will have to go to a Guitar Center to replace my bass drum pedal. For my video game. This is gonna be ugly.

Michael

Ironically, the one Bond movie I really want to hear Sean Connery pronounce was a Roger Moore one. Say it like Sean: Octopushy. Octopushy.

stevewhitaker

What's the difference between Gary Busey and fruitcake? Fruitcake doesn't always have rum in it.

thedayhascome

After picking up and bringing home literally hundreds of women at bars over the years, I can tell you this: I'll never drive a cab again.

biorhythmist

Google and me, it's like we finish each other's sentences.

rollsjoyce

Daughter asked me who was the first person ever. Evolution seemed too complicated so I went with creationism (it's the baby Jesus, right?).

jonathancoulton

I think the bird of love is the dove. My husband thinks it's the swallow.

hoosiergirl

Wow, those new iPod nanos are so environmentally friendly I think I'll buy a few extras just to bury in my vegetable garden.

mat

Does anyone else see the irony in UPS using a song from The Postal Service in their commercials?

jschoenwald

What if we find out that Cheney is actually Obama's father?

heathr

Chinese New Year is like Thanksgiving, except it's not a work holiday, it's pork instead of turkey, and there's nothing to be thankful for.

ErnieAtLYD

Wife, playing Scrabble with Mom, looking over her letters, realizing: "Jujitsu. I can spell Jujitsu." She's the Neo of Word Nerds.

tj

HEADING ON AMTRAK FROM SEATTLE TO PORTLAND. I'M LOOKING FORWARD TO REVEALING TO EVERYONE SOON THAT THEY ARE ON A SING-ALONG TRAIN.

EugeneMirman

6-yr-old nephew: "I said a bad word in my head, so I put soap in my mouth." Can't decide if this is a win or fail on my sister's part.

abigvictory

Pro tip: If your drummer isn't sweating, you need to rock harder.

MsHiss

Are you gonna kiss your mother with that mouth? Just gimme about 5 minutes here and it's all yours.

Mike_FTW

Great. There's a hole in my unicorn.

MissRFTC

The DVD of my life will include a four-hour montage of me trying to open packs of gum.

Rayke

That rehab song is gonna be a lot sadder when that poor girl fucking DIES.

alinasmith

While most people name their fists Fury or FaceSmashDeluxe, I name mine Gladys and Edna to increase the embarrassment of my victims.

emmets

Whenever you are feeling down, you can count on me to be there to help feel you up.

crispycracka

Spanish wine, English-Swedish cheese. Almost sounds like a postretirement album with Morrissey.

Kalli

Man, it's getting rough out there. Now I'm starting to despise couples in stock photography, even.

fedge

Cosmo features an article titled "How to Outsmart a Date Rapist," which is handy in light of prevailing "How to Be Date-Rape Bait" content.

kimproper

I am up, but I'll be damned if I am at 'em.

ladawn

I was inspired by today's snack, so I built a Trushiplane. It's a truck inside of a ship inside of a plane. And I just BLEW it UP.

michael_bay

Why is fertility still the default setting?

Remiel

C'mon conservatives, support your commander in chief! After all, we're fighting two wars. Three if you count the war on Christmas.

bonedaddyking

Why aren't martini glasses shaped so that they don't spill so easily on the bus?

pagecrusher

Worst-case scenario, Roomba edition: dog poo on the floor. 'Nuf said. :-(

motomike

You can't really appreciate the vapidity of most people's taste in music until you live directly above a traffic signal.

sacca

Sangria is like naughty Kool-Aid.

photomatt

Please tell your grandfather to stop sending me Evites to parties in his pants.

Hackney

Swallowed a fly earlier. I know I can get it out. If only I could remember what comes after goat.

eyeteegee

That Pixar does a great race-against-time.

Jordan_Morris

Having a tribal tattoo is like having a wallet chain that you are never, ever allowed to take off.

bluelanugo

You know what this guitar needs? Lessons.

Tony_D

The bulimic next door kept me awake all night, again. Have asked her to keep it down, but it doesn't seem to help.

nostrich

I'll tell you what. There be mad sisters up in here causing a brother to stumble. Dear Lord.

twoname

I still have a hard time thinking of NWA as an airline. To me they'll always be straight outta Compton.

margaretcho

Just had my eyes examined. Doctor says my next prescription will be a dog.

thestoryofb

Family will be here in two hours. There are not nearly enough spaces to hide things in this apartment. It's like I'm playing Shame Tetris.

zolora

A banana is a troubling thing. Because after—and ONLY after—you take a bite, it looks like a cat's ass.

disrupsean

Just chillin in the car waiting for my girlfriend but this fucking crossing guard will NOT STOP STARING AT ME!!!

fake_vincent_gallo

My God, how long are we going to have to wait for Billy Joel to write a catchy tune about the financial crisis bringing us closer together?

texburgher

Just decided I'm naming my first child "Carry-on Item" if it's a boy or "Ole Man Johnson" if it's a girl.

happyjoel

Pro tip: When you pull numbers out of your ass, try to avoid the sharp ones like 2, 3, 4, 5 & 7.

MODAT

Fact: Every time Barbara Walters makes someone cry with her first question, she gets an extra life.

gordonshumway

I accommm, I acc . . . I dood it.

ckwinny

Mr. Zoom tells me it is about time for us to go out to a nice restaurant again. We are almost out of matches for the bathrooms.

ivegotzooms

Thanks for heightening my understanding of the Arab-Israeli conflict with your inappropriately serious status updates.

someecards

Good things come on those who wait.

meaghano

NAIL POLISH DOES NOT HEAL CIGARETTE BURNS

CallMeBez

Sign on empty curbside baby crib said $10, but I swapped it for my sign that said: "FREE BABY"

McBonerPants

Things were going beautifully until he professed his undying non-ironic love for Ronald Reagan. Nothing trickled down tonight, I assure you.

fistsoffolly

I keep a record of EVERYTHING coworkers tell me. If I had a nickel for every time they told me to stop doing this, I'd have exactly $12.45.

rafitorres

A look at their remaining schedule, along with a more aggressive offense, makes me think the Somali Pirates are going to make the playoffs.

F6x

This week is so slow whoever plays it in a movie will win an Oscar.

badbanana

Once I start tooting the empty beer bottles, it's like, TOOT TOOT, HERE COMES THE PARTY BARGE! And then I look around and I'm alone and sad.

bcompton

For all its problems, the US is making progress. After 50 years, the message is finally changing from "Buckle up" to "Don't drive drunk."

whlteXbread

YOU CAN'T OUTSOURCE BALLS.

StephenAtHome

Our New York friend drives like a bad cabbie, but I can't punish him with a shitty tip.

jeffxl

I defy you to share something more humiliating than riding a recumbent bicycle in your own bedroom.

frageelay

I ain't no holla back tenor.

omgneil

1) Get ice cream. 2) Dribble on table. 3) Reach across table for napkin with which to clean it up. 4) Hey, where'd it go? 5) Dammit, boob!

vmarinelli

It's official, this economy sucks. I asked, "Can I get a what-what?" and the bank said no.

kellydeal

Saw a headline about a local teacher arrested for sex with a student. I know I should be outraged, but my first thought was, "Job opening!"

superfantastic

Oh my god, I'm a townie.

shebs

Went into Babies R Us for a gift and the salesgirl congratulated me. Bitch. Oh, and I should probably rethink this outfit.

jamield

THE LORD YOUR GOD REQUESTS AN IPHONE APP THAT GETS YOU TO SHUT UP

thelordyourgod

Dr. Drew just identified the male G-spot. It stretches from the belly button to the knees and can be stimulated by throwing a shovel at it.

erikprice

Survivorman just called, he said everyone tweeting about how cold it is can suck it. Then he made warming KY out of fish guts. Gross!

mojomaywood

Why does a 4-yr-old need a dental checkup? Aren't those teeth, like, disposable? This is like putting plastic cutlery in the dishwasher.

adamisacson

I have no intellectual equal. But I will catch up with you all eventually.

rstevens

When they both laughed at their teacher's pronunciation of platypus they thought of love. I so hate animals, he said. She touched his hand.

arjunbasu

Dating question: Should "I make my own clothes" be an upgrade or a downgrade?

fimoculous

I really wish customs agents
would stop trying to punk me.

aplusk

Always trust a coyote on where to order inexpensive contraptions. Never trust a coyote on physics.

smartasshat

My ennui is at an all-time whatever.

idvssuperego

The hotel cleaning girl just knocked on the door and came in to clean. Then said "sorry" and . . . just . . . left. Those porn movies LIED TO ME.

vhata

I cut a chunk out of my thumb at work today. HALF-DAY, BOOYAH!

beautiescandie

Just spent the better part of a 60 min. meeting trying to think of ways to derail said meeting so I have no idea what happened. I still win.

jagosaurus

Now that I own a tarot deck, sleight of hand would really come in handy.

bethylefty

One day, will our children turn to us and ask, "Mommy and Daddy, why was all of your hip-hop performed by braggy robots?"

marklisanti

I don't believe in holidays that Google doesn't change its logo for.

bengold

Candyland tastes like cardboard.

Juniorwad

I saw a guy dressed as Superman in Grand Central. I thought I recognized him but he wouldn't put on his glasses so I couldn't be sure.

trelvix

Tools for Twitter Wits

Internet comedy is serious business! These tools help you spend hours crafting a single witticism, watching your readers' reactions, and winning the approval that Dad never gave you.

Birdhouse (birdhouseapp.com): Save drafts of tweets on your iPhone.

Favrd (favrd.textism.com): Read everyone's witty tweets and see who liked what.

TweetDeck (tweetdeck.com): Separate the people you follow into groups: personal friends and entertaining strangers.

Twuffer (twuffer.com): Schedule tweets for publishing later, to spread one burst of inspiration over the following two days.

Tweetie (tweetie.com): The best way to read Twitter on an iPhone. Remember to star the tweets you like.

Is that guacamole on your pants, or are you just hap . . . That's just gross.

MamitaMojita

I like to imagine unlikely movies with Philip Glass scores. Did you know that Armageddon is a brooding and intense meditation on mortality?

phyllisstein

Walking into the 5-yr-old's bedroom and saying, "Looks like a princess *exploded* in here!" does NOT go over well with the 5-yr-old.

zuhl

I wonder how much that deficit clock cost.

susie_c

Like in "WALL•E," my first date with my wife was at a dump, then into my roach-infested apartment, where I touched her as she was passed out.

awryone

Just deactivated my
Facebook account.
I suddenly feel 25 things
lighter.

hodgman

Yoplait commercials: "This is like, approximation of my sense of womanhood by an advertising agency good."

highfiredanger

I wish I had an evil twin. Take that back, I wish I were the evil twin.

lydee

"Existentialism is a preoccupation with fear, death, and failure." I do that enough already without doing it professionally.

5dots

Both my son and my fridge have leaked onto the floor tonight. Hopefully the dishwasher isn't fazed by peer pressure.

inkedmn

Have you seen Putin with his shirt off? That is going to be a HOT war.

mulegirl

Thanks to peripheral vision and the breakfast food aisle, I thought for a moment that Post came out with a new cereal called "Just Bitches."

adtothebone

I feel like a mushroom. Kept in the dark and fed nothing but shit.

raymitheminx

I was hoping for a little more enthusiasm from this passion fruit.

sniffyjenkins

Oh, I get it, this is music that isn't to the rhythm of sexual intercourse!

Choire

I hate Freudian tits. I mean, slips.

knockout071

Sometimes there's not much difference between "manly man" and "dumbly dumb."

rongillmore

Directions on microwave meal: "Take precautions, as gravy may bubble over." Precautions? Like building a dam?

pigstubs

I'll never get a desk job. You know, when your partner stimulates you with a desk? Yuck.

Jordan_Morris

Somebody picked my dwarf friend's pocket last night. I mean, seriously, who would stoop so low?

livejamie

The bad news is we had to let go of about 8,000 clone troopers today. The good news is it really only counts as 1.

darthvader

I WAS MAILING A LETTER TODAY AND THE STAMPS SAID "USA FIRST CLASS—FOREVER." I THOUGHT, "THAT SEEMS A BIT BRAGGY."

wilshipley

Why do Christian holidays involve home invaders?
Santa, Easter Bunny . . . Jews get it. Like Passover,
the get-the-fuck-outta-my-house holiday.

joesmithreally

I guess the folks down the street don't realize that the
pointy-headed ghosts in their yard look like another
less savory kind of group.

nothlit

I don't mean to sound bitter or like a hater but OMFG
the general public sucks so bad.

megpearlz

Hamsters are great. You don't have to feed them or
give them water, then in 3 days they die and you can
just get a new one, if you want.

jakeandamir

I absolutely live for small dried fruits. They're my
raisin d'être.

drewm

Well, that's 4 movies down; the most violent one, too, unless there's something I don't know about the 40th anniversary DVD of Mary Poppins.

jzeitler

Accidentally bought scented tampons. The experience of coochie mixed w/cheap perfume is exactly what I imagine Mariah Carey to smell like.

peeppeep

For today's audition I attempted to be both big and subtle. In a word, bigtle.

JamesUrbaniak

Right now I look like the million bucks you invested in the stock market.

igotyourcrazy

The guy who invented those small touch screens on planes will experience hell as being poked in the back of the head repeatedly by pixies.

zefrank

If Great Wits Used Twitter

Twitter wit is just the latest incarnation of the timeless tradition of witty one-liners. The sharp-tongued writers of the past would have made perfect Twitter users.

Please accept my resignation. I don't want to belong to any Facebook group that will accept me as a member.

GrouchoMarxTheSpot

The only thing worse than being retweeted is not being retweeted.

GuysGoneWilde

Insanity in individuals is something rare—but in groups, parties, nations, and fans of "Two and a Half Men," it is the rule.

PeachyNietzsche

It was the best of times, it was the worst of times, so I TiVoed it for Thursday.

WhatTheDickens

Be kind, for everyone you meet found terrible parking.

AllWorkNoPlato

I'm see-through. And my top is drunk.

printartist

If "fourthmeal" is the meal between dinner &
breakfast, what is it called when you eat a kitten?

MissRFTC

The "J" on the neighbors' light-up "JOY" decoration
just burnt out. A multifaith family, perhaps?

emilybrianna

I still stalk you. I'm just not in stalk with you.

bnlandry

Cranked the treadmill up to MAX for 15 minutes.
When I finally took a break my roller skates were hot
to the touch.

thepeoplegeek

Waitress just said their creamed
spinach was "banging."
Not sure how
I feel bout that.

mshowalter

I didn't get where I am today by explaining things to retards, so either pick a dipping sauce or have your baby shower at another Chili's.

fireland

Leno criticized Twitter for having a permanent record of anything you've ever said. Sounds almost as horrible as taping yourself every day.

danielleu

Hail making scratching sounds on the windows. I told the kids snowmen were trying to get into the house. Sleep tight, kids.

badbanana

I used to complain that I had no shoes, until I met a man who threw his shoes at the president, and then I REALLY wanted shoes.

ahtitan

My mechanic just told me I could pick my car up at 5 p.m. and that they "might be having a few beers there after work." OMG is this a date?!

KatyDidSays

My personality test results came back. They're negative.

redrabbit

In suburbia, my friends say I'm one of the funniest people they've ever met. In Brooklyn, I'm just a guy without a beard.

hisnamesLen

Kudos to the Gitmo job-skills program: Those guys find work as soon as they get out.

Ryan_Durham

The baggage carousel sounds a lot more fun than it actually is.

ingridmusic

You can have my BK Cheesy Sausage Wrap when you pry it from my stiff, inflamed, gout-riddled fingers. Just take it.

sloganeerist

Razor ads for men: YEAH! You're a man! Scraping
metal across your jugular! Laugh in death's face!
Razor ads for women: Tee-hee! It's PINK!

seanhussey

Have you ever noticed that Trader Ming and Trader
Joe are never in the same room at the same time?

cockerham

"Were you exposed to livestock recently?" she asked.
"Why?" I replied. "What lies have they told you?"
Doctors don't think I'm funny either.

trelvix

A haiku is like
A poem with OCD
Now go check the stove

3hoss

At a cemetery, looking for my name on tombstones.
This is the Goth version of Googling yourself.

toddlevin

I just saved a ton of money on my car insurance by peeling out after hitting that Pinto!

kyleridolfo

That bath bomb I got as a gift was filled with GLITTER. There's got to be a less messy way to turn someone gay.

shoesonwrong

It will be a sad day in Mudville when Frankie Muniz decides he wants to be called "Frank."

busterkeaton

Michigan, the Fail-Me State

giromide

Wearing a shirt that can best be described as "lieutenant in whatever army Coldplay has started."

shellen

I'm like Brad Pitt, if Brad Pitt had a huge dick, was great at sports, and was a lot better looking.

JudahWorldChamp

Using a Q-Tip for the first time in a week must have been what Madonna was singing about in Like a Virgin.

jkottke

Uncertain times call for uncertain leadership and thankfully Congress is contributing more than its share.

willdurst

Wait. "Vagabond" means nomad? I always thought it was some kind of vaginal adhesive.

Zaius13

Holy shit! I wasn't just in a plane crash!

bobstaake

A hangover is the wrath of grapes.

Lilykily

Marble statues with a single exposed breast are the power ballads of the 1880s: every "serious artist" did one but some made a career of it.

spytap

Meth may cause "paranoia, delusions, hallucinations, which may trigger a tension headache." Jesus, not a tension headache.

rsmallbone

All the animals are on board and accounted for, Noah, but I've got bad news. The unicorns are gay.

McBonerPants

Pigs in blankets!? I never sausage a thing.

antichrista

To stimulate the economy, first we must find its G-spot.

tehawesome

My phone's predictive text just suggested "bullshit" at the end of a Valentine's text. I think it was jilted by a Nokia.

adrianadeleo

ShamWow: Beware of imitators, like the ShamMeh.

most_impressive

I wish someone would invent a smell-yourself device. That's all.

AprilSTL

John Jacob Jingleheimer Schmidt, his name is my name, too. Whenever I go out, the people always shout, "Hey . . . guy."

pagecrusher

You're more than welcome, homeless gent. However, I have to believe if you had the power to make God bless anyone, well, you'd have a home.

PBones

Discovered today that Costco sells caskets. For $799 my bachelor pad just got a bit more interesting.

snc

I like to give blood before binge-drinking to ensure maximum partying!

Ryaneustace

Jehovah's Witnesses came by today. Nice people. A little . . . "churchy."

HotAmishChick

Ran out of deodorant midway, so one arm is Shower Fresh, the other is Eastern Lily. This has the makings of a wild day.

phillygirl

Sometimes I worry I'm one of those people from the black & white parts of infomercials whose lives are held hostage by things like pockets.

luckyshirt

Where to Find the Wit

With Twitter, every little daily circumstance is a gold vein of humor that you will come to mine for years until everyone tells you to get a new shtick already. And comedy comes from more than the obvious sources. But here are the obvious sources.

1. Family: Children are to be seen, heard, and embarrassed throughout their adult lives with your detailed record of the adorable things they said as kids.

2. Work: Ever get jealous of the people who run this site? They get paid to sit around reading Twitter. If you just make sure your boss doesn't see your screen, so can you.

3. Drinking: It's not alcoholism if you do it alone but laugh about it with your Internet friends.

4. Strangers: Be polite as you want to weird, annoying, or entertaining strangers. They don't have to know they're the butt of your Twitter joke.

5. Politics: Discuss your most deeply held opinions in the perfect format for spirited conversation: a service that only gives you 140 characters to make your point. It's like holding the presidential debates via bumper sticker.

I propose every American get one free killing. We'd all be nicer to each other because you'd never know if someone had used theirs up.

smartgoat

I'm not exactly one to bring the funk, but perhaps I shall rent the funk for the day.

jackholt

OK. If you were my ambition and career goals, where would you be hiding?

glessner

James Brown didn't write lyrics. He wrote commands and instructions.

riebschlager

My haircut went from "cool" to "Christian golfer" a lot faster this time.

scottsimpson

I took the "Which meme are you?" quiz and the result is: The One Where You Photoshop Something or Whatever.

jasonpermenter

There is no ill that great sex can't cure. Except nymphomania. Then I guess you're fucked.

mayjah

When your feelings are best described by a Jewel song, it's probably time to hide the cutlery.

srslainey

Dear incredibly hot gym instructor: Thanks for wearing a Brokeback Mountain T today so I can finally stop shamelessly flirting with no ROI.

echuckles

Ratio of boys to girls at the Disneyland princess coronation—1:300. That's my Quinn.

tempo

My daughter is eating vegetarian chicken nuggets. I'll bet chickens gathered outside the lab that developed that food. "How's it coming?"

paulapoundstone

Wearing new navy-and-white-striped sweater, feeling like some kind of nautical bumblebee.

sh

Any sufficiently advanced technology is indistinguishable from witchcraft and should be burnt.

yoz

I got an extra two years just because I laughed every time the judge said penal.

Juniorwad

Legless man screaming: "I gave half my body in 'Nam & nobody will even give me a dollar." Gave him leftover Vietnamese food. Kind or cruel?

jonathangrubb

Kool-Aid Man probably felt like a total prick when he busted through that hut wall in Jonestown.

TBMimsTheThird

We've now been in our house for a week and love it. I'm going to cherish every moment between now and foreclosure.

essdogg

The baby just saw me naked. Now she knows where she got her thighs.

AuntMarvel

In the biggest Wal-Mart of my life. There's *weather* in here.

cleversimon

Acupuncture works. How many sick porcupines have you seen?

thedolittlevet

We drink coffee here like it's going out of style. When it does go out of style, I guess we'll drink it ironically.

johntunger

I was really impressed by Bush's farewell speech. He should have delivered that YEARS ago.

cockerham

Jim pointed to my 5-month-old nephew and sassily promised, "With three minutes of concerted effort, we could have one of those too."

CcSteff

When I tell people that I am a cat person, I feel like a little part of them is let down that I am not a cat-human hybrid.

LILWAYNESWORLD

Even Hemingway was a Hemingway impersonator.

mollycrabapple

Why did Donkey Kong even bother throwing barrels? Why not let Mario get up to his level and then just beat the shit out of him?

samhey

I cannot WAIT until the final episode of "ER," when the entire city develops rabies, a T. rex invades, and Clooney blows up the hospital.

emzbulletproof

Either that chick was anorexic or the coatrack just got up & walked out of the room.

kariedwards

I just wish there was a way to *monitor* Christian Science.

aedison

Eating Doritos while copying out my new weights routine, I am a mystery wrapped in an enigma dusted in florescent-orange fake cheese powder.

jaimealyse

How awkward will this be on a scale of one to threeway?

jacobbijani

My god,
if squirrels spent
half as much time
trying to cure cancer
as they do trying
to figure out
bird feeders . . .

susanorlean

Does Jack Kevorkian deliver?

alegna24

Took Myers-Briggs for first time in 5 years.
Went from INTJ to ENTJ. Basically I'm still an
overthinking douche, but I talk to people now.

homerdash

Just explained Twitter to my friend Bill. I don't think
I did it right, as he's excited to sign up.

ryanmumm

Anthropologie: The official wardrobe of Audrey
Hepburn fanfic writers everwhere.

SeoulBrother

I respect your right to express your opinion as long
as you respect my right to slowly lose interest in
whatever it is you're talking about.

apelad

Ever since my brother pointed out its double meaning, the children's store downstairs, "Hey, Diddle Diddle," has made me uneasy.

camh

Harry Potter and the Fact That 3 Students Always Have to Save the School Is a Scathing Indictment of the Tenure System.

Moltz

You answer the phone, sure it's your significant other. It's a salesman. The French call that split second of intimacy "the little rape."

ckwinny

"What's your favorite mid-range dessert wine to pair with fruit?" Boy, these password questions are getting tricky.

jdickerson

The worst thing about being an atheist is that you'll never get to say, "I told you so."

mandyjwatson

BILLY MAYS IS LIKE CAPS LOCK IN REAL LIFE.

Rayke

As if there weren't enough horrors in Nazi Germany, they were but a keystroke away from exposure to Hogan's Herpes.

rommiej

I spend the day leaving scraps of paper with celebrities' names and long numbers near different banks around the city, and I feel at peace.

midnightstories

The greatest gift you can give a child is time. Just kidding, it's probably some Pokémon shit.

johnmoe

Just bought three knives and a coffee grinder. I can't wait to see what movies Amazon recommends to me next.

itsbynnereel

Guy in fatigues in the bar looking for his buddies.
Can't find 'em BECAUSE THEY'RE IN CAMO TOO.

jimray

To those I've promised postcards: They are coming!
I will not let you down! Well, I mean, I probably will,
but in different ways.

zolora

Congratulations! You've done it! I am aware of breast
cancer!

youngamerican

Twittering "Skittles" will get you on the Skittles.com
homepage. Isn't that the most underage Latino
abortion thing you've ever heard?

samreich

"Yo, bro, explaining Burning Man is like trying
to explain color to someone who's blind." And
consequently wishes they were also deaf.

AinsleyofAttack

Got a great massage today. It's like the masseuse knew instinctively that I hold all of my tension in my penis.

DougBenson

I'm at the Bill Murray-decides-to-join-the-army point in my life.

BrilliantOrange

I like Brazilian food. You almost never find hair in it.

MODAT

Instead of writing my name on my milk jug in the office fridge, I'm going to start taping on a Polaroid of myself drinking straight from it.

Remiel

Just try and make a fist while you're holding a mango. Can't do it. You want world peace, plant mango trees.

cluckcluckers

If someone
spits gum on
the sidewalk, we
should be able
to take their
DNA from it,
clone them, and
then beat the
shit out of
their clone.

paulfeig

If I seduce it, really get it going, then leave it alone for ten minutes, maybe this paper will finish itself.

katefeetie

A Tulsa, OK, boy made a suicide pact with a well-known radio host, a pact that only one would keep. And now you know the rest of the story.

strutting

Somehow, I doubt the lady yelling, "GIVE ME MY FREE LATTE, CAUSE KARMA WILL GET YOU IF YOU DON'T, B*TCH," really gets the concept of karma.

summerjane

It seems that, no matter how ugly a place may be, it will have "Keep XYZ Beautiful" signs. New Jersey has them. Mordor probably does, too.

jonathaneunice

They said I was just like a Republican Bill Clinton. Close, but no cigar.

LameBush

I need a woman that "gets" me. Or at least doesn't think there's something wrong with me just because I organize my Beanie Babies by phylum.

Fakeweiler

I don't care what my psychiatrist says. I'm glad I'm a Jedi.

ttseco

When Lindsay Lohan and Samantha Ronson bump uglies it must look like two bicycles trying to braid each other's streamers.

AinsleyofAttack

Each time I stay at a hotel, they've found another little pillow to add to the pile at the head of the bed. It's like a pillow arms race.

zeldman

Overheard: If you torture data long enough, you can get it to confess to anything.

adactio

I get a disproportionate sense of accomplishment when I clean a speck off the mirror, because it's a two-for-one.

eyelemon

Wondering if hipsterism is catching, like the swine flu. In Williamsburg this weekend & suddenly feel like wearing skinny jeans & knit cap.

EOverbey

I'm not so sure a good man is that hard to find, but there's no question that a hard man is good to find.

ctually

I've become so cynical about advertising that, now that milk is on TV, I wonder if it really is good for you.

heathr

All this rain, and no one to look out my mansion window and sing a Top 20 (on the urban charts) love song about.

slapclap

ONCE AGAIN IT OCCURS
TO ME THAT YOU COULD
KIDNAP ANYONE BY
STANDING CONFIDENTLY IN
AN AIRPORT WITH A CARD
WITH THEIR NAME ON IT.

NEILHIMSELF

All of my creativity and motivation seems to have seeped out into the carpet, and for once in their lives, someone vacuumed it.

alinasmith

After reading about the pet chimp attack, I killed our gecko just as a precaution.

buzzblog

Oh my god. I am in the mentally ill person line at the grocery store.

molls

The baby has gotten into the habit of falling asleep while I drive us home. So at least we have that in common.

toldorknown

I'm pretty sure, almost positive, that it doesn't go, "For beautiful, oh, spacious thighs."

Tinu

Five Rules of Twitter Wit

1. Be brief. You're not writing a novel. If you are writing a novel, my guess is you should stop, burn it, and apologize.

2. Don't get too clever. You'll spend the whole day explaining your joke to baffled followers.

3. Write a draft and save it. The better version will occur to you in an hour.

4. Stretch yourself. Take a break from puns for a bon mot. Stop the insult jokes and write a limerick.

5. Relax. The next tweet will be funnier.

In addition to charging me an extra $50 to sit next to my wife, US Airways will charge $55 for our 3 bags. The CEO must have a heroin habit.

mat

NEW COMMANDMENT: THOU SHALT NOT

thelordyourgod

Some people say, "Drinking after you've just woken is inappropriate," and to them I say, "What if you wake up at a party?"

jakec

Just saw a white guy dancing and thought, "What a dork." Then realized it was a black guy and thought, "Y'know, he's actually pretty good."

ScottAukerman

Honestly, calling your paper toilet seat cover brand "Life Guard" seems a little melodramatic.

brittany

I messed up and engineered an invisible Sea-Monkey. Now I can't remember which glass is ok to drink from.

crispycracka

Open the pod bay door, asshole.

Frageelay

Just saw a bumper sticker that read, "Torture Is a Moral Issue." Whoa, never thought of it that way.

michael

Today I'm 31. That's like 80 in Facebook years.

melissagira

I just sneezed into a box of tissues, and now I'm not really sure what to do.

Rachelskirts

This cover band is playing a song where they often sing, "YOUR SEX IS ON FIRE," but at no time mention getting that checked out.

kimproper

It's so cold today that the local flasher was caught *describing* himself to women.

penfabulous

Thinking if we changed the name of "taxes" to "hookers" we might be able to get politicians to pay them.

TerryBain

Managing 3 Twitter accounts can be dicey. For ex, the other day I almost sent you guys my cat's recent tweet: "Happy to report: clean butt."

johnprocopio

You never see anyone covered in soot these days. Where did it all go?

rccoomedy

I just realized Chewbacca carries a purse.

kellydeal

Way to go, hiccups. Thanks for ruining my street cred.

sween

My decision to seek and attend the Catholic church with the best website was a little like looking for the puppy with the best GRE scores.

EffingBoring

"I did not hit you. I just high-fived your face."

brittneyg

It's adorable when Canadians try to look all pimpy with fistfuls of Canadian money. "LOOK AT ALL MY COUPONS!!!"

merkley

My kids' new Winnie the Pooh book shows they have a new human pal, a girl. So Christopher Robin finally grew up & moved to West Hollywood?

BillCorbett

The condoms I use are so sensitive, they stick around to talk to the chick for an hour after I leave.

ersatzmoe

The worst thing about "We Didn't Start the Fire" is that what finally sends Billy Joel over the edge is the Pepsi Challenge.

philgs

Chapstick should be marketed as making-out lube.

elisharene

I'm thinking about calling child protective services on Mother Nature.

DanaBrunetti

The Chinese might be beating us in the "economy" game these days, but they are WAY behind us with the whole New Year thing.

A_Brianstorm

Ahhh, the clitoris: nature's Rubik's Cube.

twoname

VH1's new line up consists of a spin-off of a spin-off, and a spin-off of a spin-off of a spin-off, which is surprisingly creative.

joebreed

In SF's city guides, events are grouped by category. Art and museums are lumped into "Art/Museums" while "Jam Bands" is its own thing.

missionmission

One of you people has stolen my brain, and I want it back raight naow bfoor tinghs gtt ny wurs

warrenellis

Ah. In that thread, "JEW" was short for "Jimmy Eat World." Editing my vitriolic reply to your "I FUCKIN' HATE JEW SONGS" comment posthaste.

youhas

I just watched a pot come to a boil and now I'm wondering what other lies I've been living.

GorillaSushi

Deriving my porn alias from my first pet's name and the street I grew up on, I'd be Munchie Hood. Pretty much guarantees girl-on-girl only.

Aimee_B_Loved

Obama was able to shower and dress after his workout in 18 minutes. His press conference was 24 minutes. May make 15-minute brownies in 12.

jdickerson

Some people don't like Vietnamese food, but I don't know what they're complaining pho.

spdracerx

I'd tell my ex to go fly a kite, but he has problems keeping things up.

hoosiergirl

Why should *I* be the
one to
take the kids to see
their psychologist?

I don't even love them **!**

fireland

Buying groceries online is convenient but deadly boring. As a result, most things in our fridge start with "A," "B," or "C."

adamisacson

I just realized all my friends are married. I freak out if I keep a Netflix for more than a week.

dascola

I think it's so great how Anthony Bourdain's cheeks waited to get pregnant until after he quit smoking.

lindstifa

No ma'am, Wireless-G isn't a rapper.

lefauxfrog

Just typed "search resluts" by mistake. Sorta makes sense. Search resluts: when all your searches bring up the same adult content sites.

johntunger

If you haven't seen
"Crying Game"

STOP
READING
THIS.

For the rest of us,
how insane was it that that
girl turned out to be a DUDE?

davidwain

Why doesn't Krackel challenge CRUNCH's
supremacy in the chocolate-and-crisped-rice space?
Why does Hershey's keep it in the fun-size ghetto?

andrewdupont

Remember, kids, it's a crime to not film sex you've
paid for.

subsocial

Physics student emailed me at end of semester,
"Are you sure I got an A?" So I changed it to a THE
WORLD IS GOING TO FUCKING EAT YOU ALIVE.

nonsequiturific

My tits look awesome when I pick them up off the
floor and put them in a bra.

fourformom

If I had a corn maze, I'd call it "The Corn Maize"!
That's probably why they won't let me have a corn
maze.

dartanion

There's a line between metrosexual and homosexual that you're walking your dog right past, sir.

tomcunningham

Mourning doves are the most common songbird in my neighborhood. And they're all horny right now. Sounds like a goddamn Joy Division concert.

sunshynegrll

Little known fact: Aquaman is peeing in the ocean ALL THE TIME.

fancycwabs

I'm giving up for Lent.

ladawn

Saw a lost dog sign for a shih tzu/Yorkie mix. He's not lost—he's hiding, afraid of what you will try to breed him with next.

zmatt

You'd think my sister's OCD & ADD would cancel out. Really they just make her forget what she's doing halfway into reorganizing your closet.

poeks

Upon seeing rampant toddler in mall: Before kid: Control your brat! After: Must plot intercept course, allowing for pull of gumball machine.

seanhussey

Allergy testing confirmed that I am allergic to everything outdoors, including trees, grasses, weeds, and reggae festivals.

gshellen

Sometimes I wish I could sing, but I ALWAYS wish I could fly.

baileygenine

The plural of vagina is awesome.

InSoOutSo

MELBOURNE, IN A DARK HOTEL ROOM. I MAY BECOME A VIGILANTE SUPERHERO, MY COSTUME MADE FROM THINGS I FIND. BEHOLD CAPTAIN SHOWER CURTAIN.

RUSTYROCKETS

Every time I see Nancy Grace on TV I imagine that somewhere there is a real journalist locked in a broom closet weeping.

shellen

My ideal hybrid: Naomi Chomsky

ttseco

Away to the window I flew like a flash, tore open the shutters and threw up the sash. Damn it, I knew I shouldn't have eaten so much sash.

shuffshuff

Giraffes are kinda like periscopes for themselves.

sippymccloy

Levi Johnston on "Tyra" is the best thing anyone has ever done, including the Sistine Chapel.

BorowitzReport

Don't say "y'all" when what you mean is "youse guys."

munki

"We're sorry; the new Facebook is back up."

busterkeaton

When the wife comes to you and says, "I think my water broke," just look at her calmly and say, "That's OK, we'll get you another one."

Robsama

God, I just LOVE the feeling of my teeth after falling asleep with a cough drop in my mouth. Like little tube socks on each and every one.

califmom

Was excited to see the "Concert Tickets" link in iTunes until it took me to TicketMaster. The Internet equivalent of candy and a rape van.

kyleridolfo

Safest way to run w/ scissors: one in each hand, the pointy ends directly in front of your eyeballs, so you can always see where they are.

sfslim

Synopsis for "Twilight": "And then, like, vampires."

giromide

Business in the front, party in the back, and floor hockey on the weekends.

grrrrbark

With all the sand my son brings home in his shoes, I think the preschoolers are working on a tunnel like in "The Great Escape."

jackholt

The normal side of me says, "Just let it go." But the frosted side . . .

NikolHasler

Business slow at Heritage Foundation's AynRandLand, where you build and operate your own damn ride or there is no ride.

pourmecoffee

I have a cold. It makes my voice sound like a sexy pirate.

joelmchale

I'm pretty sure the guy I just saw in my building is meant to be my next ex-boyfriend. He already looked so sad about our breakup.

ungraceful

Every time I turn a thousand pages to the back of "Infinite Jest," I half expect the little footnote to read, simply, "Sorry."

lianamaeby

I want to see Apple put out a Christmas MacBook made of white chocolate just so I can hear you nerds defend it.

_why

I have almost taught my dog to respond to the command "Reconsider your lifestyle."

anildash

When I play a game that allows you to choose between male and female avatars I always pick the girl. Then it's not my fault when I lose.

rossp832

Ladies, here's the deal. I have stars. You have tweets. You show your tweets, you get a star, okay? So, if you want to get back at daddy . . .

ayeshamus

Michael Jackson is 50 today. Now his face is too old to date his nose in all societies.

awryone

Just received my first McDonald's Monopoly pieces. If I can get Oriental Avenue, I'll win diabetes.

gordonshumway

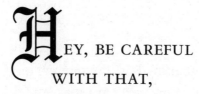

HEY, BE CAREFUL WITH THAT, JESUS HAS A PROBLEM WITH PEOPLE WHO DON'T TAKE HIM SERIOUSLY. THEY MAKE HIM A LITTLE cross.

FarkerPeaceboy

My new Chicago mantra is "It's another gorgeous day inside!"

dickc

Maybe I'm tempting fate. I'm moving on Fri. the 13th. Also picking up my new car today, and driving it to Crystal Lake for premarital sex.

toddlevin

Nothing like televised magic to take the magic out of television.

gshellen

I don't like bloody marys. Everyone says, "*My* bloody marys are different. You'll like *my* bloody marys." Is this how lesbians feel?

eliashiebert

Atheism predates any religion by about 14 billion years.

bjornkri

I think the proof there is intelligent life on other planets is the fact they've obviously chosen not to contact us.

willdurst

Mom: "My biggest regret was not being able to breast-feed you. You just didn't want my boob!" I guess that should've been a hint.

savorygreatness

Staring at a lip gloss color called Flesh Light. Not sure if I should buy it or go down on it.

suddenlybruisin

Thank you, Pizza Hut, for the world's most dilapidated $1 bill. I hope you will be serving me some Purell with this.

whitewhines

"When you die, can I have your stuff?" "You are my stuff."

abigvictory

Ending a mini vacation with a terrible cold. How bad? The stuff I just coughed out reminded me to add "Ghostbusters" to my Netflix queue.

rafitorres

5yo keeps singing, "I kissed a squirrel and I liked it. I hope I don't get rabies." I hope he doesn't grow up to be a furry.

YummyCupcakes

Buenos Aires traffic is like the tango—everyone's moving really fast and somehow, miraculously, no one gets kicked in the nuts.

teeveedub

When I fake-type on my desk and feel like I've made a fake-typo, I fake-backspace to correct it. This is my life.

kurtw

The next Bond title already causing controversy. "Pissypants Fingerbang."

Glinner

My new favorite thing in the world is when a kind Internet stranger mails me COOKIES!!! Yay! I'm returning the favor and mailing you a cat!

crispycracka

So distracted, can't work . . . am actually clicking on ads. I might have just mortgaged my wife for a free BlackBerry.

toddadamson

Was "Tom & Jerry Kids" really necessary? Was the original's dry, too-academic humor flying over anyone's head?

nevenmrgan

I appreciate that modern medicine gives us the option of penicillin instead of sending the boy to the seaside and burning all of his toys.

cjereneta

Found birth control pills and ten dollars in my dog's bed. Makes me wonder if he's running a small prostitution ring.

kellyjay7

When people pick their
"5 people living
or dead to have
dinner with,"
don't they worry they'll
be the most boring
person at the meal?

michaelianblack

Wit, n.: the delicate art of subtly steering a conversation in the direction of the hilarious pun you came up with three weeks ago.

dwineman

When I put sea salt on fish, I wonder if they may already know each other.

phillygirl

I'm to the point now where I could make the kids' lunches in my sleep. And judging by this peanut butter and ham sandwich, I just did.

stevewhitaker

I am 40, which of course is the new 17, 17 now being the new fetal alcohol syndrome.

chrisstrouth

If I had kids, they wouldn't know that batteries could be replaced until their teens.

shaggerty

If the medical profession really wanted to be dicks, they'd add a new letter to ADHD every year.

sween

I've yet to see a pair of boots that *weren't* made for walking.

secretsquirrel

The Olympics closing ceremony looks like someone gave Björk an unlimited budget and a countryful of glow sticks and said, "Choreograph!"

moonlet

Secretary pulling the ole "my alarm didn't go off" late routine. Wonder if she'll dig my "your bonus got lost in the mail."

jakepotter

I realized tonight that a Framboise Lambic is what it'd taste like if they made alcoholic Nerds. Next thought was "Oh, that's what *I* am."

jasonpermenter

What to Do When Twitter's Down

Every Twitter wit sometimes meets the Fail Whale, a cartoon on the site's error page and Twitter's unofficial mascot. What can you do when the site isn't working?

1. Check the weather, find a webcam pointed at your block, ask five other people what they're doing, then decide not to go outside.

2. Log onto World of Warcraft and tease everyone about wasting their lives socializing online.

3. Check Twitter again. IM some friends to make them load it too, in case the site's just down for you.

4. Get high and watch the news. Think up witty answers to every rhetorical headline. Hey, you could beat Jon Stewart at this game! Let's go Google his producer's cell phone.

5. Heckle the barista.

Tonight's edition of supermarket pickup lines: "What kind of apples are those?" The kind who have boyfriends.

echuckles

Around 3 a.m. I get an email from "a nice girl that would like to chat + pics." Poor girl can't afford a domain and uses only IP addresses.

kevinrose

It's my third day on nothing but bread and watery soup. Which makes this illness one unjust verdict short of a 19th-century French prison.

elizabethlittle

Doctor says I only *sprained* my pride. He advised me to stay off it for 3 to 4 days, but I'm sure it will be fine tomorrow.

tj

I'd love to see a fight between William of Ockham and Rube Goldberg.

sitemost

BUCK UP.
COLD WEATHER NEVER KILLED ANYONE.

badbanana

Even cancer likes boobs.

benmarvin

Attention inventors: Computers need faces. Nice, big, stabbable faces.

rrsotomayor

I will follow you into the sunset, in hopes you catch on fire and I get to watch.

drunkstepfather

Come on, you're canceling my gym membership for that? What about all those times I tickled him while he was bench-pressing & he didn't die?

melissasantos

Want to know how I can monetize all of this populist outrage.

BorowitzReport

His voice had a certain kind of resonance. It helped define him. So when his kid kicked him in the groin, he didn't know who he was anymore.

arjunbasu

Everyone thinks it's so cute when a cat gets on a piano, but eventually it's like, okay, we get it. You like Supertramp. Give it a rest!

Zaius13

I just got a new high score at Dishwasher Tetris!

*d_g_*

Pirate first aid: If the wound is smaller than your fist, drink rum. If it's bigger than your fist, stuff a parrot in it.

PirateParenting

When I'm whistling and someone spontaneously joins in I react as if they're helping me at the urinal.

iancorey

Overhearing young New Yorkers on a bad first date (boredly trading exotic travel plans) is like listening to purebred puppies whine.

anamariecox

Wanna know how far I have lowered the bar? 3 people have asked me what the special occasion is, because my shirt is tucked in.

Wallaceh

I just drank some scotch to take the edge off only to discover it was all edge.

ed_x

Heather Locklear looks better in her mug shot than any other photo. I guess that shows that I'm looking for things she isn't.

pennjillette

This is one of those weeks between "HOT ENOUGH FOR YA?" and "COLD ENOUGH FOR YA?" when no one in Chicago has anything to say.

phyllisstein

OMG, I'm at Baja Fresh and they have a Diablo Taco. I'm like, "Me too, IN MY PANTS."

diablocody

Not all TV shows need a holiday episode. For example, take "Law & Order: Christmas Special Victims Unit."

tehawesome

Does anyone else Twitter faster toward the end of the post to see if you can somehow fit more than the allotted characters in? It never work

JimJeroo

My VW Beetle can't deliver when I want a "GET THE FUCK OUT OF MY WAY" honk. It's all, "Hi! Let's get a latte after you move just a smidge!"

wryredhead

My idea of a trust exercise is not constantly topping off my phone battery.

rstevens

Found my 6th grade diary. Tragic or funny to see heart dotted i's in "suicidal"?

NikolHasler

Lady. Say "You're welcome a lot" in response to my "thanks a lot" one more time, and we're gonna be in the newspaper tomorrow.

beep

How delicate, how fleeting our hold on nuance and subtlety, on the conversation that stirs our hearts and minds, when my butt itches.

texburgher

Sometimes I like to imagine that my BlackBerry shoots lasers.

joshu

What's that, Dreamy TA? Your wife is an engineer too? Is she one of those engineers that DON'T EXIST CUZ I LIVE IN A FANTASY WORLD LALALA?

omgneil

Hemingway: "For sale: baby shoes, never worn."
Me in high school: "Twelve-pack of condoms, never used."

zuhl

Paris is the Paris of things that other things are the thing of.

dwineman

If you're bisexual, naturally, people ask about your relationship status like you're pregnant. Boy or girl? Hopefully once, you say twins.

jomoto

Who are all the cab drivers talking to on the phone all the time? Other cab drivers?

skidder

Diaper change epiphany: corn can't possibly have any nutritional value.

irreverend

Two people are arguing just outside as to the definition of a "glancing blow." Do I really have to do everything? Here. Let me demonstrate.

trelvix

I'm immune to your accusations of homophobia.
Some of my best shirts are gay.

Moltz

True Tolkien devotees have of course read his
masterwork, "The Favicon."

zeldman

Pet review: cat collar bells. Easy to care for and feed,
but you may need to buy a cat to tell where it is.

TheAmazingKim

I just love walking. I guess you could call me a
pedophile.

domnit

Jewish kids have classes on the ways people have
tried to kill us. Latest cause? The length of the
classes.

clapifyoulikeme

ABOUT TO GO ONSTAGE IN PORTLAND, OR! TALK ABOUT A BUNCH OF WHITE DEVILS. WISH ME LUCK! MIGHT HAVE TO CALL SOME-ONE W/ A TAN "BLACK"!

LisaLampanelli

Whole lotta begatting.

HotAmishChick

There is nothing more infuriatingly depressing than a stale fortune cookie.

jagosaurus

Son fell asleep on the couch watching "Nemo," so I paused it on the sharks and scooted the couch within 6" of the flat screen. Now we wait.

InSoOutSo

No insurance, so I've self-diagnosed based on movies: tuberculosis. I hope it's the pretty Nicole Kidman TB, not the sweaty Val Kilmer kind.

superfantastic

PSA idea for DC motorists: "Honking and You: Practical vs. Wanton"

gschueler

If I am able to finish this tweet, then this is the slowest cashier in the world. Dum dee dum. Ba ba ba. Do do do. La la la. Gleep glop.

seanhussey

I think people are more violently opposed to fur than leather because it's so much safer to harass rich bitches than motorcycle gangs.

LucyRcardo

If a bitch is a bitch (Ice Cube), and bitches ain't shit but hoes and tricks (Dr. Dre, Snoop Dogg, et al.) we can conclude bitches is magic.

SeoulBrother

So now Blagojevich has been double-impeached, which sounds like a Ben & Jerry's flavor.

earlkabong

If I were an OBGYN, my catchphrases would be "At your cervix!" and "Not guilty, Your Honor."

detweiler

Two pregnant women on the bus. It better not be contagious.

munki

When Morgan Freeman reads a book, whose voice is in his head?

bonerparty

It's cool how we can go from "hooray, racism is defeated!" to "those cunning Japanese devils" over just 2 weeks of newspaper op-eds.

FrSpike

Go ahead, say "Fat Tuesday" but in 15 years, successful Tuesday's going to friend you on Facebook and you're going to feel like a huge jerk.

GorillaSushi

Just knocked a Twix loose from the vending machine with sheer brute force. As usual, the entire office pretends to be unimpressed.

erikprice

Hey, is it considered molestation
if the child makes the first move?
I'm gonna need a quick answer on this.

SarahKSilverman

I used the L-word. But I made sure the squeeze was almost asleep first, so I could later argue that it was just a dream.

sarahdopp

When you have kids, "treasured heirloom" and "smells like pee" are not mutually exclusive.

gknauss

Now that everyone knows who the 5th Cylon is, I can't get into the best restaurants anymore. So much for celebrity.

hodgman

I will not consider you my "pal" until you send me my money, PayDick.

angleofattack

Ever fall asleep reading Wikipedia and wake up feeling totally disambiguated?

alisonrosen

HIV testing at work today. They make a special point to say "no needles!" because when you get an HIV test, the needle is the scary thing.

topherchris

Crutches are cool if you think of them as Auto-Tune for walking.

scottsimpson

I really feel sorry for the people in "Lost." They still have four more years of Bush to deal with.

KuraFire

You never know what I have up my sleeve. Today, for instance, it was a green bean.

MsHiss

I have a lot of writing to do today. Imagine that I'm saying that with a gigantic smile. Also, for the hell of it, put me in a top hat.

redrabbit

Your baby did not appreciate my Pacino impression.
I don't know, he crawled outside somewhere. Yeah,
well, maybe my FEELINGS got run over!

fireland

Just bought a watch on sale that's water resistant to
100 m, so if I ever find myself down that deep, I'll
know what time I died.

adtothebone

5yo pointing towards disposal in ladies' restroom: "Is
that where girls put their coupons?"

emzbulletproof

I love this shirt. I love this coffee. I just don't want
them hanging out together.

girlnamedcaptn

French Connection clerk was so goddamn smarmy I
wanted to tell him to go fcuk himself.

printartist

If I could sleep with any celebrity, living or dead, I would.

oldblinddeadjim

Premise: Computers are horrible. Theory, from premise: As phones become tiny computers, their horribleness will increase in kind.

al3x

You never really appreciate how much stuff fits inside a Costco-sized container of something until you spill it.

ericspiegelman

They have all these cases for the iPhone but not a single one that I can wear as underwear.

ShawnaF

California Update: We apparently don't have any water. I guess people won't really start to panic until we run out of silicone and collagen.

Ryan_Durham

History shows the Japanese were only able to destroy one US city after the bombing of Pearl Harbor: Detroit.

byx

I am so homesick. So I've pretty much stopped going there altogether.

delfie

I never have a problem keeping "Christ in Christmas," as I'm sure to invoke his name several times Christmas Eve assembling the kid's toys.

joeschmidt

Packing for my buddy's bachelor trip in New Orleans. No idea what one wears when "clubbing," so packing my "douchebag" Halloween costume.

dens

I'm not saying that it's the best, but if there is anything better than hot, freshly baked banana bread, I haven't had sex with it.

DieLaughing

Made it rain

at the club last night.

Thought people grab all the money

and give it back

so you can throw it again.

Not how it works

I guess.

azizansari

At lunch with my daughter. This girl makes the best wingman. Where was she when I was single?

luckyshirt

Rice is a good option if you feel like eating 3,000 of something.

*badarama_*

What my proctologist doesn't know yet won't hurt him. Might surprise him, though. Teehee!

rolandfox

I've always relied on the kindness of strangers and the hatred of loved ones.

yuribaranovsky

Apparently the act of combining DNA from two adults with ADD can result in an eight-year-old with the personality of a pogo stick.

vmarinelli

Her: "So what do you do in NYC?" Me: "Lunch." Her: "No, really." Me: "Really. It's a city of lunch."

fimoculous

New term for today: "bone juice." "I have to wash the sheets today. There's dried bone juice all over them."

expat_erin

"These people are not aware of my awesomeness. I should probably lean out the window of my limo and screech."

jkubicek

Boss affectionately referred to the 5th and 6th shots of tequila as "team building." By end of day we could have started a sports league.

bethylefty

I came down with a case of veganism last week, but the doctor gave me some cream for it.

TheAmazingKim

The Epic Fight

One of the most annoying yet compelling uses of Twitter is live-tweeting: a sort of embedded reporting from Twitter. In this example, the user blissfork tracks a series of epic fights she's overheard from her neighbors.

"I don't think a rock on a metal band is worth thousands of dollars, but YOU do. YOU convinced me that it's worth it. But now I wonder."

"I want to marry you? That's like saying I want to go to the museum. When I'm fucking stoned all the time my feelings don't match."

"All I have wanted for YEARS is for our engagementship to move forward. All that I want is you. All that I HAVE wanted is you."

"I TOLD YOU NOT TO FUCKING DO THAT! I TOLD YOU I AM FUCKING LEAVING YOU! I DON'T LOVE YOU! I DON'T WANT TO MARRY YOU!"

She must really want that engagement ring. She just gave him a blowy in the living room.
blissfork

On a scale of 1-10 how pathetic is it if I go out alone? Ok, well, how about if I take off this shirt that says, "Looking for a baby daddy"?

frostinglickr

Anyone else get paranoid as a kid thinking that they may not have said "amen" at the end of a prayer and that God was still listening?

caseymckinnon

Just spent 3 min trying to bite open tea packet, mumbling motherrrrfuckerrrrrr. Tea bag dangly thing says, "Let your manners speak for you."

JBRabin

I want to open a gym called House of Reps.

friedmanjon

I love how reading dating profiles gives so much insight into a person's past lovers, like "NO CHEATERS!" or listing meth as a deal breaker.

furrygirl

Passing the Apple Store iPhone line I thought, "Camping on the street in San Francisco seems so cool, people should do it more often!"

jacksonwest

If plungers could talk, you wouldn't own one.

swamibooba

An extra DVD about Hitler isn't exactly what I'd call a "bonus."

bsheepies

I like having fun with my facial hair when I shave. Right now I've got a half chinstrap, one mutton, and a toothbrush.

eyeteegee

I'm getting too old for this. Soon I'll need each of you to remember what you did to piss me off. Maybe write it down, pin it to your coat.

Mike_FTW

Just trained my daughter to shout,

"Help, this isn't my daddy!"

while walking hand in hand down the street.

Glinner

I wonder what would happen if I mailed my landlord a check for $1 less. This could be the beginning of a very dangerous social experiment.

willandbeyond

Really, those Virgin planes look so much like a bad club you expect the stewardesses to roofie your in-flight beverage service.

marklisanti

Three-Card Monte Python is when you get taken for $60 and then a 16-ton weight is dropped on your head.

A_Brianstorm

Rain! Is spring close? Or is God sad because snow touches itself?

jordonm

"You will not sucks forever." Thanks, fortune cookie.

pheend

I want smooth-jazz-canceling headphones.

disrupsean

Nearby house is painted bright yellow. Don't mind that, but they missed a patch. Some night I'm going over with a box of highlighters.

smartgoat

Sex. Me. This burrito. Pick any two. Wait, stop, I was going to eat that.

rommiej

Burned hand on popcorn, jumped in pain, knocked knife off counter, stabbed foot, got paper cut from Band-Aid wrapper. Take that, Darwin!

jamield

I have, for now, successfully dodged the question of whether Elmo has a "wee-wee."

mikemorrow

A friend msgd me a picture, "africankids.jpg." When I closed the msg, it said: "africankids not saved. Save now?" I have God's cell phone.

ersatzmoe

Overheard at Wal-Mart: "How many gift cards with the Asians on 'em did you get?"

tylercoates

I like to play a game when I people-watch. I call it "Girlfriend or Daughter?" It's not really the kind of game you win.

cleversimon

Daughter uses mouse to drag scrollbar. Me: single tear.

jonathancoulton

My grandpa walked in on me playing GTA IV. "Yeah, Grandpa . . . this is, um, just a driving simu—whoops. What? Oh, no. He'll be fine."

SuperSanko

Still a little bitter that Yahoo! didn't go with my suggestion of "Fuckin' A!" at the naming meeting.

FarkerPeaceboy

Dreamt I was playing a combination of GTA and Wheel of Fortune. I shot a hooker, took her money, and bought a vowel.

chowbok

There's no use putting it off any longer. I'm going to have to revise my will, and specifically define which Muppets get what.

bearskinrug

We just diagnosed a kid on "House" with the Chronic Uglies.

schmutzie

Richard Littlejohn is an English journalist so committed to bigotry that he would probably forcibly repatriate Santa Claus to Lapland.

rustyrockets

Who would win in a fight between dinosaurs and Transformers? I know what you're going to say, but not all Transformers turn into a dinosaur.

bnlandry

My new excuse for leaving the bar early on a Saturday night: I gotta preach tomorrow.

jimray

As much as I love Sondre Lerche, watching him try to rock out reminds me of my little cousin playing w/ my Fisher-Price guitar.

Aubs

There is a certain amount of information you can gather about a country by how straight their legs are when they march.

saidme

Not sure what's more amazing: the fact that the geese are all so horny, or that they can read my bumper sticker in the first place.

smilinbjones

You know, most of the Harry Potter book plots would be over in 3 chapters if they had a decent search engine.

kevinmarks

For a guy wearing a "Silence is Golden, Duct Tape is Silver" tee, you sure don't ever seem to shut UP.

hotheadred

Got small shelf at work with prewritten answers to common questions I get. Now, I can just say, "Let me pull an answer out of my Ask Rack!"

EffingBoring

Eating an entire frittata. Note: Devise method for making half a frittata.

Adrianchen

If you obsessively brush and re-brush your teeth like I do, raise your hand! Now raise your other hand to keep things even!

emilybrianna

Back from HeightWatchers.
Disappointed. I've put on five
inches. Plus, I smashed my face
on the doorframe.
Might start smoking again.

serafinowicz

Amnesty International sent an e-mail with the subject "Duncan Sheik's coming to your hometown!" Funny, I thought they were against torture.

alexlitel

Saw "Slumdog Millionaire." Number of families who left after the first 30 minutes: 1. Number of kids who may be scarred for life: 2.

jschoenwald

PSA: "Instant coffee" isn't either.

johntunger

Recession Update: I'm down to one burrito per paycheck. I have neither the energy nor the pico de gallo to joke about this.

essdogg

How can I construct an outfit that is equal parts "bend me over" and "I think we would have an incredible relationship if you stuck around"?

kades

I don't trust the Easter Bunny. I think he's been hiding something from me.

mrraygun

Local SimCity player has no fucking clue what that adviser is talking about, new report shows.

dbecher

Call it luck or stupidity, but every time I play the dispenser game in the gas station restroom I win a flavored balloon.

thedayhascome

Well, the good news is that now I know what poison ivy looks like.

robot_operator

CODEPENDENTS OF THE WORLD, UNITE!! Now promise me you'll never leave . . .

adangerlove

rainnwilson **{** The word "scone"
perfectly describes what it is.

I wonder what it's like for a rock 'n' roll saxophonist before work. Knowing you're going to go in there and just ruin everything.

johnmoe

The thing about taking a day off when you are a stay-at-home mom is that then people call it neglect. Except, of course, in France.

LidMo

The way McCain talks about earmarks reminds me of when my grandfather gets cranky when his salad doesn't have enough tomatoes.

jomc

Sometimes I stub a SnackWell's out on my arm just to feel less alive.

highindustrial

Swedish is infinitely less spooky when translated into English.

sashafrerejones

Got to therapy early today only to catch her with another patient. "You're doing this just to spite me!" She booked me through 2009.

Mike_FTW

It's nice that they're loaning me a lead vest to protect me from the X-ray machine at the dentist, but the gun pointed at my face.

ev

My boss's dog has been barking for 2 hours straight. I think she's saying, "Something something Timmy something hurt." I don't speak dog well.

brienis

So I have this friend, right? She's exclusively into guys with well-defined buttocks. So she only makes passes at chaps that aren't assless.

strutting

I like to think that all the heavy sighs at work are just people letting the enthusiasm out.

gknauss

Even with a cup full of change, the hobo wouldn't front me $.50 to add vanilla to my latte. Hope the bastard has fun finding his cart.

buttahface

I love spending time with my 6 nieces and nephews. One at a time. Because all of them at once is enough to make me want to torch my uterus.

essentially_me

Watching American Music Awards. I am too old for the Jonas Brothers. I am too old for the Jonas Brothers . . . Maybe not that middle one.

rachelsklar

Sometimes it's like my wife and I aren't even related.

samhey

Some days you get the bear. And some days you conspire with the bear to fake your own death and move to the beach.

swimparallel

This guy has such a narrow soul patch I thought he had a run-in with a black Sharpie.

ChiNurse

A friend was just diagnosed with Bob Hoskins disease. It causes crippling obscurity. I barely know who she is anymore.

dickchiclets

Everyone always says how sweet babies are, but it's a little known fact that babies also stay crunchy in milk.

FanEffingTastic

Well, yeah, the traditional calendar says it's the 8th, but if we're going by my chocolate Advent calendar, it's totally the 22nd already.

gretchasketch

People who live in Los Angeles spend about 1/3 of their day looking for parking. Fortunately the rest of the time we're kissing celebrities.

Just_Alison

A 10-YEAR-OLD KID JUST YELLED "LICK IT FOR TEN" AT ME. OH MY GOD, WHAT HAVE I DONE?

jimmyfallon

The most pessimistic sentence possible: "Rainbows are shaped like frowns."

dangurewitch

I just learned that the moon was in the 7th house last week, AND Jupiter just aligned with Mars. Now where the heck did I put my freak flag?

LeoLaporte

I wish a radio station would play "I Got You Babe" on repeat every Groundhog Day just to fuck with people.

magnetbox

It's ALF you want to spend a night on the town with, but it's E.T. you want to go home to.

kapto

You know you're in a dry spell when your encounter with a turnstile nearly has a happy ending.

ronbailey

He said, "Over my dead body!" and I guess I see now that it wasn't polite to ask if I could pencil that in.

msteciuk

The tomato is the tranny of fruit.

MelodyMcC

Slept terribly last night. Do they have a pill for Restless Vagina Syndrome?

sokeri

Yes, I call that dancing. I have rhythm. I have LOTS of rhythm. I was just using it all at once.

yowhatsthehaps

Wine has calories? What the fuck?

fourformom

If I lived every day like it was my last, I'd probably just have a lot of parking tickets.

torrez

The planning stage is my very favorite stage. It's so pleasantly distant from the failing stage.

Maggie

It's -13F out and your midriff-baring coat ensemble makes you look like a whore. Got any plans for the weekend?

whlteXbread

I would never want to be able to read people's minds. Imagine all the Mariah Carey songs I'd have to wade through to get their ATM PINs.

timdawks

Do you think the Man with the Yellow Hat mentions George on his Internet dating profile?

maritzav

Just FYI a lot of parents don't dig it when you grab their kid and say, "You're my Bonus Jonas" while you gently caress their hair.

paulscheer

I don't want to be abducted by the Greys anymore if they're not going to buy new magazines for the anal probe lab's waiting room.

stevehuff

Maybe if I look like I'm going to shoplift, I can get help in the Electronics section at Target.

practicalwitch

For all the things I've achieved, I can't shake the notion that my life has mostly been spent converting breakfast cereal into body hair.

phylhrmnix

It must have been great to grow up on Hoth. "School's closed again today, kids."

mogrify

To do list for the day: hate self, love self, hate self, love self. Lunch. Hate self.

michaelianblack

WANT TO BE AS FAMOUS AS SUSAN BOYLE!

hirstdamien

Success means being the last one connected to the conference call.

AaronKaro

I'm going to start referring to babies as "crypods."

nerdist

Contrary to popular belief, you don't lose any energy, stamina, or potency when you hit 40. It just all gets channeled into your nose hair.

Weirdsmobile

The 250lb girl wearing Danskins in my spinning class has officially graduated from cameltoe to mooseknuckle.

primalpurge

What my proctologist doesn't know yet won't hurt him. Might surprise him, though. Teehee!

rolandfox

I stood there wondering, "Why is that Frisbee getting bigger?" Then it hit me.

Notactuallyme

For Mardi Gras this year, I'm giving up beads.

favecock

I don't think it matters what your beliefs are, but praying about your laptop choice is a little much. God doesn't care which Mac you get.

ECByrd

Toddlers come up with the cutest names for things. "Schindler's List" is the Choo-Choo Movie.

Balut

Analyze a friend's relationship just by looking at pics on Facebook. You can see the precise moment his new GF says, "Fuck it, I'm eating."

indefensible

How to give a great handjob. Step 1: Use your mouth.

myracles

I really enjoyed my youth. I don't know why I told him to go home to his mom.

blondediva11

Teach a man that you can't be trusted to use a fishhook and you'll effectively have taught him to fish for you for life.

Shakin_Atoms

I never tire of songs that explain the differences between women of different geographic regions in sexual terms. They're educational.

thejoelstein

It would really suck to be the guy who discovers Live Strong bracelets cause cancer.

nictate